FEROCIOUS FIGHTING ANIMALS

TASMANIAN DEVILS

Julia J. Quinlan

PowerKiDS press

New York

Published in 2013 by The Rosen Publishing Group, Inc.
29 East 21st Street, New York, NY 10010

First Edition

Editor: Amelie von Zumbusch
Book Design: Andrew Povolny

Photo Credits: Cover Tier Und Naturfotografie J und C Sohns/Photographer's Choice/Getty Images; pp. 4–5 Dave Watts/Visuals Unlimited/Getty Images; p. 6 John Carnemolla/Shutterstock.com; pp. 7, 9 (top) Jason Edward)/National Geographic Image Collection/Getty Images; p. 8 Patsy A. Jacks/Shutterstock.com; p. 9 (bottom) Tim Collins/Shutterstock.com; p. 10 Peter Parks/AFP/Getty Images; pp. 11, 17 Brendon Thorne/Getty Images; pp. 12–13 Susan Flashman/Shutterstock.com; p. 14 bumihills/Shutterstock; p. 15 John Cancalosi/age fotostock/Getty Images; p. 16 Mark Newman/Photo Researchers/Getty Images; pp. 18–19 Ted Mead/Photolibrary/Getty Images; pp. 20, 21 Danita Delimont/Gallo Images/Getty Images; p. 22 Martin Zwick/age fotostock/Getty Images.

Publisher Cataloging Data

Quinlan, Julia J.
    Tasmanian devils / Julia J. Quinlan.
    p.   cm. — (Ferocious fighting animals) — 1st ed.
Includes index.
Summary: This book tells about Tasmanian devils, marsupials found only on the island of Tasmania, including their habitat, how they raise their young, and how they got their name.
Contents: Meet the Tasmanian devil — The island of Tasmania — Furry but not cuddly — Baby devils — Ferocious Tasmanian devils — Lone wanderers — Carnivorous marsupials — What would eat a devil? — Endangered — Saving the Tasmanian devil.
    ISBN 978-1-4488-9674-5 (library binding) — ISBN 978-1-4488-9806-0 (pbk.)
ISBN 978-1-4488-9807-7 (6-pack)
    1. Tasmanian devil—Juvenile literature   [1. Tasmanian devil]   I. Title
        2013
    599.2/7—dc23

Manufactured inthe United States of America

CPSIA Compliance Information: Batch #W13PK5: For Further Information contact Rosen Publishing, New York, New York at 1-800-237-9932

CONTENTS

MEET THE TASMANIAN DEVIL

The very name "Tasmanian devil" sounds scary! Tasmanian devils got their name from European explorers. The animals' frightening shrieks and bad tempers reminded the explorers of devils in stories.

Tasmanian devils live only on the island of Tasmania. Tasmania is part of Australia. It is located off the southeastern coast of mainland Australia.

Tasmanian devils are **marsupials**, just like kangaroos and koalas. They carry their young in pouches. Unlike koalas and kangaroos, Tasmanian devils are vicious **carnivores**. They show their sharp teeth and growl when they are threatened or fighting for food. These small marsupials are truly ferocious!

Tasmanian devils let out their shrieks and screams when they are fighting over a meal with other devils.

THE ISLAND OF TASMANIA

Tasmania is not very big compared to Australia. However, it has many **habitats**. There are rain forests, grasslands, and **eucalyptus** forests. There are also beaches.

Tasmanian devils can be found in all of Tasmania's forest types but are most common in the island's coastal woodlands and open forests.

Tasmania is home to many animals and plants that live nowhere else. At one time, an animal called the Tasmanian tiger lived there. The Tasmanian tiger was not actually a tiger. It was a carnivorous marsupial, like the Tasmanian devil.

Tasmanian devils once lived on the mainland of Australia and other islands nearby. They now live only on Tasmania. Tasmanian devils live all over Tasmania but like to be by the coast or in forests the most.

This devil is crossing a tidal flat. Tidal flats are areas along the shore that are sometimes covered by the tide. They can be good places for devils to find food.

FURRY BUT NOT CUDDLY

Tasmanian devils are not very big. They can grow to be 20 to 31 inches (51–79 cm) long. Their tails are about 10 inches (26 cm) long. Devils weigh between 9 and 26 pounds (4–12 kg). They have black or brown fur. Many devils also have white patches or stripes on their chests or sides. Devils are very stocky. They have large heads with very strong jaws.

Tasmanian devils can open their mouths very wide.

Devils have four toes on their back feet and five toes on their front feet.

The Tasmanian devil has one of the most powerful bites of any animal.

Tasmanian devils make a stinky smell. They use this smell to scare away other animals.

Tasmanian devils' back legs are shorter than their front legs.

9

BABY DEVILS

Tasmanian devils are marsupials. Marsupials are different from other **mammals**. Marsupial babies are very tiny when they are born. The newborn babies crawl into their mothers' pouches. They stay there and drink their mothers' milk until they are big enough to come out.

After they have come out of their mother's pouch, joeys often ride around on her back.

10

Tasmanian devils can have up to 50 babies at once. However, no more than 4 will survive. Female Tasmanian devils have only four teats for babies to drink milk from. Baby Tasmanian devils are called joeys or pups. Joeys come out of the pouch when they are four months old. They leave their mothers at eight months old.

After her joeys have left her pouch, a Tasmanian devil mother will go off to hunt on her own. The joeys hide in a den until their mother comes back.

11

FEROCIOUS TASMANIAN DEVILS

Tasmanian devils often fight when they see each other. Males fight over which one gets to mate with females. Females fight off small males that want to mate with them. When several devils find a meal, they fight over who will eat first.

LONE WANDERERS

Tasmanian devils are most active at night but do like to sit in the Sun sometimes. They spend most of their time alone. However, male and female Tasmanian devils do come together to mate, or make babies.

Scientists have found that Tasmanian devils tend to stay in a den for between one and three days at a time.

Devils make many noises, including snorts, coughs, grunts, growls, and screams.

Tasmanian devils live in dens. They make their dens in burrows, trees, or caves. Tasmanian devils travel around a lot and have several dens that they live in. Scientists believe that they keep the same dens for their whole lives. They have home ranges, or areas where they roam. Their home ranges cover an average of 5 square miles (13 sq km).

CARNIVOROUS MARSUPIALS

Tasmanian devils are mostly **scavengers**. They often eat dead animals. They feed on sheep, cattle, and other dead animals that they find. Sometimes, Tasmanian devils come together to feed on the **carcass** of an animal. They will also eat trash that people leave behind. They hunt small mammals, reptiles, and insects, too.

This Tasmanian devil is feeding on a wallaby carcass. Along with wombats, wallabies are the devil's favorite food.

16

Tasmanian devils have very strong senses of smell. They use their noses to track down food. Their strong teeth and jaws bite through bone! When Tasmanian devils eat an animal, they eat the whole thing. This even includes the bones, hair, and **organs**!

Tasmanian devils can eat 40 percent of their body weight in half an hour.

WHAT WOULD EAT A DEVIL?

Before they died out, Tasmanian tigers hunted Tasmanian devils. Today, adult Tasmanian devils do not have many predators. Eagles and owls will catch and eat young Tasmanian devils. Sometimes, larger Tasmanian devils eat smaller devils. Younger devils climb trees to escape older, larger devils. The larger devils are not as good at climbing as younger devils are.

When devils are threatened, they make growling sounds. Their ears may turn bright red when they are excited or angry. If they need to fight, devils use their sharp teeth. Devils are more likely to run away than fight, though.

Bigger Tasmanian devils are among the few animals that Tasmanian devils need to fear.

18

ENDANGERED

Tasmanian devils were hunted almost to **extinction** by early European settlers. They did not like devils because they thought they were eating their **livestock**. Now, devils are protected.

Even though Tasmanian devils are no longer killed by humans, they are **endangered**. Many Tasmanian devils have died from a sickness called Devil Facial Tumor Disease, or DFTD.

Scientists in Tasmania have been tracking DFTD's spread. This scientist is releasing a devil he checked for the disease back into the wild.

A scientist is checking this devil's mouth for signs of DFTD. Devils that get the disease die because they are unable to eat.

Since scientists learned about the disease in 1996, the devil **population** has gone down 80 percent. Doctors and scientists are trying to find a cure for the disease but haven't had success so far. The devils get sick from biting each other.

SAVING THE TASMANIAN DEVIL

The people of Tasmania and the rest of Australia love Tasmanian devils. Devils are one of the symbols of Australia and Tasmania. People are working hard to save the Tasmanian devil. Unfortunately, their future is not looking very good. Hopefully, scientists will discover a cure for Devil Facial Tumor Disease.

Most people think Tasmanian devils are dangerous and crazy. However, devils are not dangerous to people. In fact, they are an important part of the **ecosystem** of Tasmania.

Tasmanian devils keep the forest clear of dead animals by eating their carcasses.

GLOSSARY

carcass (KAR-kus) A dead body.

carnivores (KAHR-neh-vorz) Animals that eat only other animals.

ecosystem (EE-koh-sis-tem) A community of living things and the surroundings in which they live.

endangered (in-DAYN-jerd) In danger of no longer existing.

eucalyptus (yoo-kuh-LIP-tus) A tall, evergreen tree that grows in warm places.

extinction (ek-STINGK-shun) The state of no longer existing.

habitats (HA-buh-tats) The kinds of land where animals or plants naturally live.

livestock (LYV-stok) Animals raised by people.

marsupials (mahr-SOO-pee-ulz) Animals that carry their young in pouches.

mammals (MA-mulz) Warm-blooded animals that have backbones and hair, breathe air, and feed milk to their young.

organs (AWR-gunz) Parts inside the body that do a job.

population (pop-yoo-LAY-shun) A group of animals or people living in the same place.

scavengers (SKA-ven-jurz) Animals that eat dead things.

INDEX

A
Australia, 4, 6–7, 22

C
carnivores, 4

E
explorers, 4
extinction, 20

F
forests, 6–7

H
habitats, 6
humans, 20

I
island(s), 4, 7

K
kangaroos, 4

L
livestock, 20

M
mammals, 10, 16
marsupial(s), 4, 7, 10

N
name, 4

O
organs, 17

P
population, 21

WEBSITES

Due to the changing nature of Internet links, PowerKids Press has developed an online list of websites related to the subject of this book. This site is updated regularly. Please use this link to access the list: www.powerkidslinks.com/ffa/devil/